Giraffe
on Fire

CAMINO DEL SOL
A Latina and Latino Literary Series

Giraffe
on Fire

JUAN FELIPE HERRERA

The University of Arizona Press

Tucson

The University of Arizona Press
© 2001 Juan Felipe Herrera
First Printing
All rights reserved

06   05   04   03   02   01   6   5   4   3   2   1

Library of Congress Cataloging-in-Publication Data
Herrera, Juan Felipe.
Giraffe on fire / Juan Felipe Herrera.
p.   cm. — (Camino del sol)
ISBN 0-8165-1985-4 (alk. paper)
1. Mexican Americans—Poetry.   I. Title.   II. Series.
PS3558.E74 G57 2001
811'.54—dc21   00-009732

British Library Cataloguing-in-Publication Data
A catalogue record for this book is available from the British Library.

Publication of this book is made possible in part by the proceeds of a permanent
endowment created with the assistance of a Challenge Grant from the National
Endowment for the Humanities, a federal agency.

Poem by Li-Young Lee from "The Cleaving," © 1990 Li-Young Lee. Reprinted
from The City in Which I Love You, by Li-Young Lee, with the permission of
BOA Editions, Ltd.

Always for Margarita of the wise eyes.

See how this shape
hoards itself, see how
little it is.
See its grease on the blade.
Is this how I'll be found
when judgment is passed, when names
are called, when crimes are tallied?
This is also how I looked before I tore my mother open.
Is this how I presided over my century, is this how
I regarded the murders?

—Li-Young Lee

Tabla de Materias

Acknowledgments

Gracias to *Ergo!, The New England Review, The Bloomsbury Review, Touching the Fire,* and the *American Poetry Review* for publishing a number of these texts in their earlier versions. Patti Hartmann, Marvin Bell, Ray González, Arthur Vogelsang—thanks for walking these poems out into the wild and peaceful air.

Your Throat Burns, Red

Your Throat Burns, Red

—For Bob Hedley, Shelly Berc, and Tish Jones

Riding my bike in the black machine-gun night
caressing the soft sidewalk
the melting shadow
the marshy shadow
I gallop through this borderland
this Hyacinth sky . . .
—Joshua Ryan, from "Riding My Bike in the Black Suburban Night"

Set: Open desert. Parking lot. Subway. Surgery room.
Speaker(s): One voice. Many voices. Displaced. Looped. Off stage. On stage.
Prerecorded. Live. Women. Men. Nothing. Naked. Hidden. Fully dressed in
Elizabethan fashion. Military fatigues.
Movement: Explosive. Devonian.
Sound: Missiles. Car crash loop. Tango. Sighs, giggle. Rain. Fire. Prison siren.
Sloppy cafeteria eating.
Plot: None. Invent.
Extras: Paparazzi.

Your Throat Burns, Red.

Your throat burns, Red.

Body
and bones spin out
to the big yards.

You spin off toward different horizons
kneeling, seated, lying down, crouching
you drive the iron—lift them weights,
invisible
you write on the wall
where there ain't no wall
the universe
the fat wall, girl—falling up.
A vertical ocean.

You be in the black box. Now. Your hands
scratch your face. You walk. You run
full speed—on the double. With the eyes turned up
frantic speed. Possibly blind. Can't speak
Just a bit. Stammering.

In the black box. Now. Your hands
scratch your face. You walk. You run
full speed—on the double. With the eyes turned up
frantic speed. Possibly blind.

Get up—get down. You have a knot in the throat
Red. The wide knot. Pushing. A stone. Suffocate, sucker.
You explode in screams.

Your bones. You break. A branch
something inside—snaps out.
You can't cover your mouth
weeping. Grotesque.

Dream it up, sucker. A fucking bird.
Put up
your arms. Slowly. Change it. Change it.
Fly. Fly.

Into the crowd. Moan if you can.
Let them hear you. Moan. Scratch the wall
sweat—cry out, intertwine. Intertwine
untouchable. Gasp, sucker. You
crazy hard you trapped
in the boxcar
remember, invisible—the wall
it presses you—home girl;
so you try something. You
beat against it. The wall. The big box.

Against it
that cube of space. Dense.

Move it girl. Move. Move. On with it!
Tie yourself to the others. Jump
into the flesh knot. On up with it.
Explode against the wall. The big wall. Your shoulders
your back. They're going to bash you. Sucker.

Even if your bones snap out. Your eyes.
Scratch the box. Transparent. Move it.

Slowly your blood will weaken.
You get sick, sucker. Rot. You rot.

Cough it up. Rot. Piss rot.
Smell rot. Hospitals
you'll be dying, sucker, girl.

You can't take it huh? You crackin'.
Crackin'—can't hold it huh?

The others stay indifferent.
The others give a shit. You
jump them. Yes. So you jump.
Turn on them, into them
their greasy skin, pebbled
violent skin of bodies
the paralyzed ones
swallow them, home girl
swallow them. Jump.

Everybody's laughing it up. You
stink! You animal. You begin now,
spin fast. Spinning. Chasin'
your tail, sucker. Against the wall.
The guard. The yard. Fat guard
in fatigues in the office
no ducats here, big girl.
Men machines. Women machines.
A typewriter. Silly woman.
Snapping. Clicking.
Clickety-clicking!
Snapping—spitting, sucker!
Listen to the hiss.
Over on the wall you find something
a calendar. Check it out. What time is it?
Machine time.
Machine time.
Say it.
Sucker girl.
You pronounce the name in growling
long high vanishing voices.

Your eyes go up.
Oh, yes they do
up.

You twist your eyes. Slowly. Open the gate.

And a thousand keys—Go for the chair.
The body-chairs.

You grope for the body-chairs. Sucker.
You
get old fast.
A cup of coffee for the old woman.
That's it.

Can't control the fingers.
The fingers smeared with rot.
You drop it. So you kneel down.
Way down sucker.
You won't be able to hold anyone's hand.
Useless now. Pick up your rot.
Your useless arms. Come on.

Pick up your cup of rot.
The grass howls. The grass rots.

Won't be able to hold anyone's hand.
Useless now. Pick up your rot.
Your useless arms. Come on!
Pick up your cup of rot.

Just the yard, man.
The grass stiff. And you.
You sweat a certain cold film.
It sticks.

You squat. You look for a cigarette
in the bag. Reach for the wallet.
Lean, home girl. Lean into the light.
A photo. You pick up a photo. A handsome girl.
You bring it close to the eyes.
You lose it. You lose it
in the dirt.

You grab it in the air. You try,
you say. To revive, you say.
If only to revive,
you say.

You want it in your hands
but you lose it in the dirt.
You want it in the hands
so you open them.
Until they burn in your eyes.

Fly with your little hands. The pretty photo
up there somewhere—gone. You break down.
You bend. The head. The eyes. You walk it.
Lost in triangles. Sucker girl
The wall will surprise you.

Remember?

In the face. You sweat.
You are determined
to knock it down. Sad girl! Come on,
knock it down! With your ancient arms
with your veins. You fly, sucker
you're free. Yes. Finally
you are free.

Fly up. Then. Stutter fool
Happy girl—you hit them
you jump, keep on jumpin'
stammering with happiness
as far as you can—hit the others
a wall—again, sucker. A round
stinking wall. It will compress
you into the center of the world
to push you

to press you
to close you down. Break you down,
Fool.

An iron knife blossom.
Feel it beating and buzzing.
You want out?
The flower will pulse.
You want out?
Fall in then. Sucker. Fall
in then. March. March, I said.
You are a solemn army of gray
banners. Lift up
your little gray banner.

Blow!

   Blow!

I said you are free, sucker. You're free.
Jump. Spit the rot. Blow,
come on. Take off. Toward the universe.
The wall
will meet you. Push it.
Drag it a little ways

into you. At the center of the yard
open
close
the iron blossom knife.

The columns advance. Marching.
Closer—spitting rot. The column splits—
one side with machine guns. Aim
at them. They join ferociously.
Aim, sucker. The hungry. The rot,

the heroes, the courageous,
the stutterers.

Fire on them, come on.
With their guns, the army beats
on the dead. The army snarls.
They
yap
yap
yap
yap
yap
yap

Yap madness
celebrate madness. Tell them.

Look out!
Between shrieks of laughter
someone listens—the army smells
it—so they aim, they advance
perhaps toward someone
they follow.

They wake up. Even the dead
wake up
sometime, sucker. Listen.

They drag themselves
along with their weapons
they empty them
against the army
they kill a few, just a few
with rapid fire the army
finishes them off. Wiped out.
Easy. Except
one. Just

one.
They wake up.

Even the dead wake up
sometime, sucker. Listen.

They drag themselves
along with their weapons.

To burn her.
They execute her with rapid fire.
You wake up from the dead army rot
and you cry, sucker!

You cry
for her.

Look at them,
closely.

Walking away
kneeling
bent. You are alone now.
Still crying over
the body. Mourning
the corpse—you feel
a hum in the air. Rot.
Prayers. You abandon
the body. You
abandon her.

Bent. You are alone now.
Still crying over
the body. Rot.
Prayers. You abandon
the body. You
abandon her.

Something in the air
so much of it—speed up.
The humming speeds up.
Take a few steps, now.
Run.

Run after the others.
Moan. Scream. Shout, sucker.
Fall on your knees. Scream
look at them
pound the walls
with their
little fists

the walls of invisible columns.

Look at them fight it. Smashing
their weapons against it. Against
everything. Bloody bones.
They lift their eyes.
Shoulders
Arms,

suckers.

Little by little. Look at them.
Hug the wall. Curl up their thick thighs.
Their spit. Their biceps—their rags.
Their rot, their suede, their rot kissing the wall.
Their rot kissing their rot. Look
how they smile. Pat each other
on the back. Look at them console themselves.
So.

You try to free them—sucker, girl.
You shout. You throw your wasted body

at the universe with your arms
flying up.

Smashing
their weapons against it. Against
everything. Bloody bones.
They lift their eyes.
Shoulders
Arms.

Suckers!

Little by little. Look at them.
Hug the wall. Curl up their thick thighs.
Their spit. Their biceps—their rags!
Their rot, their suede, their rot kissing the wall.
Their rot kissing their

rot!

Just your eyes now.
The black rings inside you—the wall
will burn. Yes. It will burn up, now.

The invisible wall will be humming—up
above you—over
you.

Your throat burns, Red.
Body and bones spin out
to the big yards. You spin off toward different horizons
kneeling, seated, lying down, crouching
you drive the iron—lift them weights, invisible
you write on the wall where there ain't no wall
the universe
the fat wall, girl—falling up.

A vertical ocean.

They wake up. Even the dead
wake up
sometime, sucker. Listen.
They kill a few, just a few.

Except
one. Just

one.

They burn her.

They execute her with rapid fire.
You wake up from the dead army rot
and you cry, sucker.
You cry

for her.

Bull and Octopus
(Adiós, querido PRI)

Monday: nothing

nothing only nothing and fists—full of veins
shawls in ambush delirious over your mask
your lie you (Yes) you Minotaur-boy tell us
of your towers Amerindian (only) you tell us of this little
blind-eye dog battle that you leave us and now in this
lake of our own violet shadows you want
us to receive your guild your ribbon and dinner jacket
for a toast in a glass
on a plate architecturally yours yours
Amerinothing of your great lobster hands like this
you want us

Monday: I am

I am
bullet-riddled inside Skinnybone Martínez the one with
                    overhauled rage Chiclets Boy (pocket bloated
now, stretching) Yes
just like the gum stuff old mandible sputum—
Cabeza de vaca Head of a woman weeping a desert of hands
bullet riddled and one thousand (5) thousand mothers of a dead boy, a girl
Lily flame (her name is Señorita Solitary Ash;
his name Fire Without a Hungry Altar Without a Leaf)—fast flame,
tiny dagger, little wrist doll in the thick coffee barracks
crazy tin shrapnel sky shred

Monday: (PRI jet)

(PRI jet) This is the string—this is the noose
this is the brown slashed head, the lost knot, the holy twine,
twisted head, headless—the dream of _____
the new dream of man-handkerchief artificial ice
iodine tank Christmas: suppliant supplicate suppliant
positions (he says)
     in the mass graves in the building with shoes and bandages and sweets,
coconut and carpets on sale and pumpkin seeds and confetti
in the stone rubble volcanic ash .

Monday: (No)

           (No) you want me like this (sob) only like this
Here (Look) ebony ribs moons Tlatilco-like Usumacinta-like
Antofagasta-like Tlaltelolco-like and there
you ask in this late infinite afternoon for bread and wine
—repose and return,
(compositions by iron and blasts) because you wanted me
in your foreign jet fruit tin and knee casket
and the woman (you said) with archbishop hands
folded in your name (you said)
bricklayer legs and cheekbones
that mounts dark stone, fire and lime
in the house of the foreman—you want her bricklayer

Monday: —you

—you want her hung open your linen cloth
No I don't talk nor will I speak (of G——) nor will I complete his name
Anyway—it's just you
        I judge you—like the orphan and poet (that I am)

Monday: I

I judge you here I
demonstrate and I send you Goya's tunic octopus
skeleton and head shortened stolen
Villa, the Northener's mask
the one searching for you and one thousand Adela Zapatas and
Tehuanas Kahlo with an eye on the forehead with swollen candles
and your grayish flesh tambourines
—these workers bakers sweet candy twisters the mechanic
Siqueiros Segundo from the corner with your carburator wire
he's going to pinch the lungs
in the morning and María Tepache chuckles at the banderillas
already inside your pulpit's artificial leg your bed and
students from the province read and destroy, read and destroy and
city students read you and destroy you
in your friar's holy spirit shell that you
created for democracy
head of jewels fabricated through television owl sets
Americani rage and this tiny girl mute mouth of Sebastián thorned
and this floor inundated with horns and flames breaks your face

Monday: Still

Still
breaks your face—from the stirrups from the crutch
from this winter-spring from the worker's barn
tragic and melancholy fictions
breaks your nose with my sand,
with our shadow, with my Huichol woman orphan frying pan
and kindling wood with lice and splendor lizards here
you come even though you don't want to—toward my womb,
toward this quickening mound at fast gallop toward
my pencil toward my hunger my solar razor and you don't lose the chain
and you tell us of your lights and I look at you
take you apart on your very own shore.

**Pulpo y Toro
(Adiós, querido PRI)**

Lunes: nada

nada solamente nada y puños de venas
asaltantes rebozos delirantes sobre tu máscara
tu mentira tú (Sí) tú Minotauro-muchacho dinos
de tu pabellón Amerindio (sólo) tú dinos de esta pequeña
batalla de perro tuerto que nos dejas y ahora en este
lago de nuestras sombras violetas quieres
que recibamos tu cofradía tu listón y esmoquin
para brindar en vaso
en plato arquitectónico tuyo tuyo
Amerinada de tus grandes manos langostinas así
nos quieres

Lunes: soy yo

soy yo
bullet-riddled inside El Flaco Martínez de rabia usada
               azúcar Chiclero *boy (pocket bloated,*
now, stretching) Sí
como ese mismo chicle mandíbula vieja de bilis—
Cabeza de vaca Cabeza de mujer en llanto llano de manos
acribilladas y mil (5) mil madres de hijo muerto de hija
azucena llama (se llama Señorita Sola-Ceniza;
se llama Fuego Sin Pobre Altar Sin Hoja)—llama fugaz,
puñalito, muñeca en cuartel de café espeso
hojalata *shrapnel sky shred*

Lunes: (avión PRI)

(avión PRI) *This is the string—this is the noose—*
this is the Brown slashed head, el nudo perdido, la piola sagrada,
cabeza torcida degollada—el sueño de _____
el sueño nuevo de hombre-pañoleta hielo artificial
tanque de yodo Navidad: *suppliant* suplica *suppliant*
positions (dice)
     in the mass grave en el edificio de zapatos y vendas y dulces
coco y alfombras de barata y pepitas y reiletes
in the stone rubble volcanic ash

Lunes: (No)

(No) así me quieres (sollozo) sólo así
Tengo (mira) costillas de ébano de lunas Tlatilcas Usumacintas
Antofagastas Tlaltelolcas y allí
pides en esta tarde infinita pan y vino
—descanso y retorno,
(composiciones de hierro y fogonazo) porque me quisiste
en tu caja ajena de avión fruta lámina y rodilla
y la mujer (dijiste) con manos de arzobispo
dobladas en tu nombre (dijiste)
piernas y rostro de albañil
que monta trigueña piedra, lumbre y cal
en casa de mayordomo—la quieres albañil

Lunes: —la

—la quieres desentrañada abierta tu mantel
No hablo ni hablaré (de G_____) ni completaré su nombre
Al cabo—solamente lo tuyo
        a ti te juzgo—como huérfano y poeta (que soy)

Lunes: te

te juzgo aquí te
enseño y te mando la túnica pulpo de Goya
esqueleto y cabeza truncada robada
Máscara de Villa el Norteño
que te busca y mil Adelas Zapata y Tehuanas Kahlo con ojo
sobre la frente con velas hinchadas y panderetas
de tu carne gris
—estos trabajadores panaderos charamuscas el mecánico
Siqueiros Segundo de la esquina con tu carburador de alambre
te pinzará pulmones
al amanecer y María Tepache se burla de las banderillas
ya van sobre la pata artificial de tu púlpito tu cama y
estudiantes de provincia leen y derrotan, leen y derrotan y
estududiantes de centro solamente
te leen y te derrotan
en tu fraile cáscara espíritu santo que tu
creaste para democracia
cabeza de alhajas hechas por televisores buho
la ira y esta niña muda boca de Sebastián espinada
y este piso inundado de cuernos y llamas te rompe la faz

Lunes: Aún

Aún
te rompe la faz—desde los estribos desde la muleta
desde este invierno-primavera desde las estancias
trágicas y melancólicas ficciones
te rompe la nariz con mi arena,
con nuestra sombra, con mi sartén de huérfana huichola
y ocote, con piojos y bellas lagartijas aquí
vienes aunque no quieras—hacia mi vientre,
hacia este monte ondulante a galope hacia
mi lápiz hacia mi hambre mi calor navaja y no pierdes la cadena y
nos cuentas de tus luces y te miro
y te destrozo en tu playa misma.

Ofelia

Ofelia in Manhattan, Circa 1943

Girl, you couldn't sport a finer gabardine jacket
with Ofelia Robles going up to the sunrise service
on Easter Sunday at the Radio City Music Hall.
You see, everything was in the shape of a fancy guitar—
even the question mark by her telephone number
in my pocket calendar or the last note scribbled
on a napkin full of your philosophy.
It was all personality, black coffee, and music.
You were there, sister. Drinking post prohibition.
Even the most fancy accountant loved gospels
and occasionally visited the Methodist Broadway Temple.
I can just see it. I never forgot the staging
with that elegance of romance and rosewood;
so many notes curled in there, kind of velvety,
bow ties that you couldn't see, but
they were there, fluttering with a mysterious
sweetness at the center. That's when cousin
Tito played string bass; small, plump, hot-tempered,
polka-dot vest and on Saturdays nothing
but congas with Ralph Gómez, the No. 2 man
because he always stuttered.

In the middle of Central Park,
I was the girl with the baggy corduroys doing a tango.
Me and Ofelia and her Portuguese accent.
She was the only real dancer at 40 degrees
north latitude, baby.

I wanted the war to end. Japan had to lose, right?
The Queen Mary was serving cocktails
and you had ten in small paper cups while
we were waiting in line. Look at the sea, you sang.
It was spitting up pure imagination and ambition.
Flashes as far as the eye could see. Take the Rockefeller Center

beyond ol' Sixth Avenue, for example.
Who lived there anyway?

I just wanted to love Ofelia on the rooftops.
Rum-colored bandannas. Our open shirts.
You could hear all the busboys gripe from up there.
Bad tips, the boss that didn't like you using the phone
in the back room. A few bashful tenor voices by the jukebox.

You were reading the *New York Times* in those days.
Pretty good English.

Going like this:
Oye, que tú, esta cosa está caraja
and Mr. Pickett won't pay me as much because
I don't belong to the golf club; you know, like Wilfredo?
Everyone should live in an oyster bar, right?
That's my philosophy, sister. You used to say
that it was about purpose not just Wall Street.
That's when subways had class. And mink too.
All the women were wearing it. Ofelia looked like a doll
until Jorge, the janitor at the new Woolworth Building
told her the fur was a mutation. She gave me
some binoculars she had gotten at an auction.

Move your fingers and just like that
you could see everything. A thousand miles away, easy.
You could count all the electric peanuts in the sky,
Jesus, that's when I was still trying to get a job
working at the night cleaners. Girl,
you could even eat those sizzling candies
hanging over the park.

What about Sammy Hall,
the guy we used to box when we were kids?
He was pure muscle. Then, a fat badge.

One evening I saw him twirling his nightstick.
The guys used to grunt that he was the only black cop.
You had to be German or Polish, maybe Italian,
if you wanted to be a policeman. And that was it.
Sammy didn't like me teasing him about his floppy cap.
Man, it was just me and Ofelia. "Dizzy legs,"
I called her one night at the Rooster
listening to a little bit of Harlem royalty.
You went there, right? We were "dracula,"
the two of us, in a class by ourselves.
Girl, the clubs were hot. But, I had to move.

It happened so fast. One day I just couldn't
sell anymore of my bullfighter paintings on the street.
Nobody was buying them, anymore.
Maybe something was going to happen.
All of a sudden nobody wanted bulls
and gallant lean men in shimmering bronze suits
on their walls. People started talking about
abstract portraits, squares and upside-down eyes.
How could you eat with that stuff over your head?

Things were changing, I guess. So,
I left. Just like that. It was always about leaving paintings
and some clothes and taking paintings and some clothes.
This time, I didn't know what to take. I am telling you.

I never saw Ofelia again.
Maybe she's still dancing out there.

She had a gift you know. We said
we wouldn't write letters.
It couldn't work that way with us. It had to be pure chance.
A bird-of-paradise in a vase over a piano top, the way
Ella sang or Uncle Vince roughing you up
with his famous question: how's misery?

You said you could handle it. Just wait—
things were going to get a little better after the war.
You said someday you'd get in touch
and we'd joke about that saxophone
we put five dollars down on at the pawnshop.

I can still see the open case from here,
against the glass, a miniature city of mad sparkles,
so alive, I could step in there, dance to the music,
look sharp forever. It was our island, girl.

Shawashté

I am coming back to the fiery humor of Mexican towns, I've been dragging
a topaz-colored branch my mother gave me—flickering, since
the early years, I've been dragging these curly papers filling with light
at noon the navy yards from the west and the smoke looms up, this oil
and green steel where you lose flesh in one swing—one handsome swing
from the young jackhammer—this was Woody Herrera's death in '64.
What could they do with the stump figure and his peach-checkered leg?
Where did they bury his son's curses? Where did he walk?

I went through the tiny veins, through the cobblestone
back to El Colorín, eighty miles east of the Pacific in central Mexico.
I was asking for salt. At times, I was even more simple and
received the sharp sweetness; the kind you get from a Mexican lime
and if you are lucky from your own eyes as you gaze across the streets
full of ring vendors, Indians and fancy melting cars. I went inside.
I wanted to touch the belly under the waters—darkness opening up
a black fan with amethyst sparkles where the face was. I even slept
in a shredded hammock; the wet insects dropped from the ceiling
to click their jaws, go up again—scale the ruins.

There was a Ferris wheel with a Spanish girl wearing a pearl necklace;
the background—roses and chrome. There was a spattered bus leaving me
in the town plaza of Guatemala City—I had to fight for a ticket south;
I wanted to go deeper. The Indians crowded to see me, looking down
at the ground. Their feet were swollen, but they carried a *shawashté,*
a walking stick, blackish and stonelike, finished like a clarinet,
a clarinet of resentments. In El Salvador, that's how far I got one year
I lived on a *finca* with a robust zookeeper, a plantation man who dressed
in fatigues. I never knew his name. We drank wine once. Once, at dinner
we sang *Adiós muchachos, compañeros de mi vida.* Everyone in Latin America
knows this song. Then, I climbed up the volcano, the hills and met
the workers and their fenced-in vegetables and their love for oranges
right after they are picked, sitting cross-legged, maybe warming

tortillas on the embers, they are the ones I love the most, they are the ones tied down to a boot whose shadowy strings follow me.

I had written two pages about this. There is nothing memorable, nothing here, the publishers said. I kept on, going through my oversized clothes. My color was somewhere between a burgundy and a brown; passions consumed me, I think—something between a burgundy and a brown. My cheeks were hollow, my hair, oily, longish to the midback. I wore muslin and *huaraches*, the type the tourists buy—not meant for wearing because they are pointed. I was a clown of sorts. I strayed, at times I joined others—a Chicano from East L.A., with green eyes, a kind cameraman who kept on, now he lives in Brazil, there were others: tall women and some men with notebooks, sketchpads—they were writing too, they talked about their grandmothers whom they never met, they talked about El Paso and the Juárez border, they mentioned shame, they mentioned water. These were the tillers and scrubbers, they said, these were the prayers

for the little ghost in the grasses, for the two-headed calf
for the feeble kid, frozen with a tiny leg
for the braids inside a plastic back from the pharmacy
for the daughter walking ahead, past the terrible gates
for the husband made to drink gasoline by the patrol
for the American officer with one eye.

We camped under an old tarp and ate sweet dough baked over a wire. It tasted like licorice and rice. We shuffled backstage, put on pebbled masks, we called it the *Theater of Freedom*, and used other words too, like *teatro*, and *carpas*, for years we performed in the tobacco collectives in northern Veracruz, and back in Hollenbeck Park, in East L.A., where my buddy was from, even in Chino Prison, on the West Coast too. The inmates asked us to take cartoons and letters back to their wives. One time we went to Granger, Washington, up north, I had never seen the snow, so powdery, with lights, I grew up in Southern California. Who's to say what I'll see next, I told them. My words were spontaneous. I used words like *rebozo, lotus,* my favorite animals were the deer and

the eagle. The others used words like *bronze* and *nation* and phrases
like *viva la mujer,* there was something behind all this, free from
bitterness, in the shape of a harp, behind us.

This was 1968, this was 1974, no one cringed then, no one whispered,
we walked out of our houses and crossed the street as if underwater—
you couldn't see our eyes or even the way our hands were shifting,
the language was unknown—you could feel the heat waves though,
maybe, something traveling, rushes, fragrance, this was 1979, maybe
some are still going, I heard Carlitos Robles took his children to Italy,
Parma, they said, and Dolores Valencia made it to Berlin, every day,
from the bitten walls—she makes sure she takes the old signs down,
she says, and she puts up something from the backpack, a soda cup,
maybe with pieces of pumpernickel for the birds, a funny little meal
under the sky. I am picking a small meadow, ahead—two bushels
of bright reddish leaves in a basket, a Greyhound depot on the other
side, forlorn, with a foolish clock, it is late spring, I can tell it is a
Mexican town, by the smoke and the women's laughter, more smoke.
All morning I've been hearing tiny currents rushing through the trees,
I am walking alone, more with my left than my right, like my father.
There is much work to be done, he would say, so many ruins
to sweep, so much blue dust to settle.

Giraffe on Fire

MAP OF FIGURES

[These figures may be read with the following in mind, or the following may be read with these figures in mind]

Prophets
    Gala, Dalí's lover
    Chucho el Roto, escape artist
    Velázquez, the painter-keeper
    Chávez, leader of the Obraje
    Zapata, the seeing child
    The Tallensi warriors
    García, minstrel

The Trinity
    The Frida
    The Georgia
    The Gertrude

Counts
    Count Santiago de Calimaya
    Count Regal
    Count Valenciaga

Inquisitors
    The Consulado
    Pedro Moya de Contreras
    Hitler

Martyrs
    Cortez
    Malinche
    Freud
    St. Lara
    St. Salazar

Benefactors
   Zumárraga
   Artaud
   Don Luis de Carvajal
   Erzuli

Colonies and Territories
   Portus Acapulco
   Auschwitz
   Rwanda
   Orange Free State
   Vladivostok
   Prague
   Chiapas
   Port Ligat
   Veracruz

Forests
   Lacanjá
   East Los Angeles
   Ocosingo

Caves
   California
   Ensenada
   Kalimba
   El Infierno
   Orizaba

Plazas
   Tlaltelolco
   Phoenix
   Tiananmen

Offerings
 Amaranth
 Cochineal
 Cinnamon
 Parsley
 Garlic
 Balché
 Duck sauce
 Pámpano
 Coriander
 Pulque

Sentinels
 Kerouac
 Dalí
 Van Gogh
 Cezanne
 Dufy
 Thelonius
 Tjader
 María Félix
 Goya
 Zappa
 Lao Tzu

Tribes
 Tlaxcalans
 The Roseworkers
 Moors
 Ilongot
 Criollos
 Hmong
 Jews
 The Sausalitos
 Aztec Macehuales
 Cocopá, Sisters of the Pacific

Deities

Ocelotl

Godadavida

Sarajevo

Siwanava

The Madonna of Port Ligat

Yahwe

Ceiba

Mirages and Apparitions

La Infanta

El Paso

The Land of Kerouac

Cibola

California

Chambers of Torture

The Residence of Count Santiago de Calimaya

El Obraje

The Friars' hallway

Mysteries

The Great Speaking Stone

Smoke of the Tepo Drum

Giraffe on Fire

I

I sit on a gold vestibule. It isn't me.

This wavy swan to my naked left comes up to my bad eye. My dead eye.
Catalonia, in its sacred and tiny voyage under the tectonic plates of Dalí's
edible sea. Swan's talons. Cobalt blue and geometric. Gold pearls and an
inverted eggshell. My childhood, my little red daily missal, my edge of
Plexiglas water. My breasts and my shoulders are sculpted and small. I raise
my leg as I hold an invisible oblong figure in front of me. It is my gaze.
Naked as Gala, Dalí's lover. I know nothing. Nothing of Spain or its green-
mantled skies. I live in a split sky. Yellowish without a sun, yet the sun
envelops the firmament. The bottom is blue, then convex with a woman at
the center. Mexico. Cortez. Malinche. East Los Angeles. San Francisco. El
Paso, yes, the gate of all Mexican dreams—this soft animal, jagged with
ragged dots behind its back that leads to a holy shrine. A wax cross always
before me. I sit upright. Floating, my head tilted to the left. This is the
proper stance in America, an adequate sexual crust that I eat as I ascend
into the sky. It is not necessary to understand what is below me.

You must open your legs. You must figure the hard orange colors from
your bill, then the black protrusion. This is innocence. I was born there. A
fortune was discovered on my skin. My mother took me away one night.
An egg was delivered, then tossed over a bridge. It cut into the waters, a
shape of a man with tinted skin and a jelly heart. What could he do? He was
alone inside the small canoe. What did he have? He had paints and a loaf of
pumpernickel. He wanted to reach down into the water. The belly below
him, floating up. Gala in white, in seaweed, in parables from Ezekiel and
Port Ligat. Gala was elsewhere. Above him, as always. In front of him. As
always. In a shrunken room dug into the bowels of a West Coast barrio.
The barrio was insignificant. The fragrance was central to his existence.
This is my language. There are no codes. She sits there. That is all. In
eclipse. In fission. Hiroshima, Iraq. The San Joaquin Valley. In leather rubies
and grape pesticides. Alive and willing, still. She is traveling sideways, onto

Desolation and Desire. Avenues, voyages ripped from Cádiz and Cadáquez.
Moors and Jews come to her.

This was my beginning. In the fields,
lost in the deserts of California. Many years ago.

2

I always dreamt of holding up a champagne bottle, etched and intricate as an embossed Finn manuscript. This is not a dream. I am to one side. The left as usual. You cannot see my arm or my destitute mouth. There is a giraffe on fire. Tlaltelolco shadows purge the sea before us. Both of us. Remember Tlaltelolco, the ancient city of Mesoamerica where they carried Quetzal plumes and married Indian goddesses with chocolate, where the military dropped a helicopter of shame and grenades, helmets and ratchets on the open skulls of the peasant students?

Go to the right. The anus comes at you. The apple entices you. The chalice with wide ceramic lips and a pearl-like shadow calls you. But first you must drink from my glass. Even if I am not holding it. There is more interest in the brain. In New York. In Toledo. In Lorca's bubbling grave; the brain is the master. Parsley. Cauliflower, a vaginal swirl, gray matter between your chest, in Huichol Indian Morse codes. In red. Cutouts from my spleen.

The Consulado wants this. Wants to taste, wants to eat freely. Wants to tilt the table and plea for a flat samurai sword. Destruction tastes better with a hanging cherry. A riot in the center of things gone awry. A tin-colored mantle juxtaposed next to blackness. Velázquez sees this and smiles. I smile. I am the one crying. Wine and anise, cerulean blue drops on my wrist. They stand for a shred of sky, perfected by the whore priests on your corner. You don't call them that. You have changed your terms, you have learned the art that Goya admired. The somnambulant one-eyed terror over our houses. War. A cock and a hummingbird full of mercy. The cloth, the smock of my childhood.

3

Hold up the right corner of the sea, pleated. Lift it and find pleasure snoring, cut open by crystal and stone. Look down at your shadow by the sands, by the gilded whiteness of your legs.

Below you:
a wrapped hydrogen scarf, an ink cactus stuck to the dry galaxy below the sky veils. Touch down. Come to the ground, the talc, this desert—peeled and washed by distant clouds. My hair reddish, down to my jaws. When will I blow the conch shell? Shall I awaken the sleeper below? Who is he following with eyes closed? The perfume is solar. My nakedness is simplistic. As the sleeper searches, I find America rising on his back, mottled, brownish. Above the water, the stone folds, clutches itself, peeks through holes and rivets. We are playing. All of us, then just one. The sand has been swept with a wide brush. The girl—pensive as she lifts the folds of the water. One hand. One arm and on the other the conch shell waits. Poised.

I know the stone is the secret. The secret in the shut mouth. When I was five I cut my fingers. I cut off my thumb. I delivered ice on the back. Wolves sang from the mountains. Julián, the violin man next to us, in the Mexican village paced his floor. Julián knew his wife, Jesús, was shaking and another man was raising her hair.

4

In Veracruz, young men roll naked on their backs. On cement. On the sadism of America. They pick up their ragged shirts off the ground and receive proper tribute from the tourists: Palms, guanábana, pámpano fillets in black sauce from San Andrés where Agustín Lara learned the formula for sadness and rhythm. Where he learned to back up limousines so they could connect all things in the universe. Here is my cut jaw he said. Here are my tavern strings, he crooned as María Félix kissed the scars on his neck.

St. Lara.
I keep his candles burning. I keep oil and obsidian by the wax figure; I tell the story to the lost ones. Follow the shark tooth of the Malecón where gay Veracruzanos smoke black Tabasqueños. Whisper into the old men's bar rooms at the Hotel Ortiz. Sell fat prawn and one hand of rock salt. I was born there. I was betrayed there twice. One woman from Sinaloa suffering from rape and alcoholism. An angular man from Harvard. Caught in a tight habit of perfection and Marxism Leninism. I was alone there. Full of music and marimbas, lavish shade, the young hands of dead prisoners on the Isla de Sacrificios. I stood there. Awakened for the first time. In the tombs, the cells and the drip water from the soft arch above me. I went down into the underground labyrinths, El Infierno, black Spanish dungeons wet with phlegm and urine. A corner where I could breathe.

I tunneled up and saw nothing.
A shaft of light.

A rectangle two hundred meters above me. Every day the sun dripped for seven seconds. Then I rolled up my arms and punched myself in the testicles, so I could feel a coolness travel in a star shape through me. So I could kiss the ground with my entire body, feel the rumble from below. So I could leak into the gravel and the torn pages and knotted sheets, so I could reach for the green trousers of Chucho el Roto, so I could escape with him to Orizaba where we would climb the mountain by Jalapa. Where we would go up in November, on the day of my mother's birth and seek wisdom from the herb women. The ones who toss fire and change their breasts into pearls, ascensions, and healing stones.

5

The gold triangle is my enemy.

It speaks with Chaucer's heart, rattles on about the English penchant for redemption, about the necessity for virgins in the time of holocaust. Calls me in a fake Pakistani accent, so I can take up my woman's vest and gather my sisters. I am coming from the left side, in my mother's white gauze, in my aunt's last handful of nickels. A circle of women climb above the mountain; Frida's again, Gertrude's, and Georgia's. The hand of a man wants to follow but he cannot. The Macehuales and the new Viceroy have sent the cadaver of Cortez back to Mexico City. In Seville, they grieve him, in Catalonia all is quiet, all is sacred. I am in love with Hera. I am reading the glyphs on her belly, tarnished coins with the face of Socrates. My thighs are muscular. Her skirt is shredded by my heat, by this ablution I make every Sunday morning. It is time to begin the inquisition, they are saying.

Behind me. The men are crawling and speaking in broken Aztec. They are saying the mulattos will win this war. They are afraid that the new God at the center will speak and stand on his mutton legs. Raise my cup and toast to Georgia. Raise my shadows. I walk on bone stilts to the mound where they dance. The earth is conical today. Angles and labia. Woven calf muscles. My head goes down. See that my womb is split and a red jacket reaches into me. Out of me. Bat wing. Testicles. Ovaries and cymbals in ash-colored clouds.
Hide my face.

Take my eyes for nipples and suck. I want to carry this chair of hives and dancers. I want to solve these Spanish numbers. A brown blue, a gold fleshiness. Only the bust in the cave remains peaceful.

6

When I entered the cave I found Velázquez. Was he dying? Was he asking for one more Infanta? Where is Margarita? He asked me. Where is the black hive above the hills to mesmerize me? A torn page came down. A figure of a woman in the fifties. She wore a reddish skirt and lay on the ground. But her head was full of lines, swishes and trapezoids.

A cigarette.
I could barely see the cigarette. The inquisition handed down by Pedro Moya de Contreras had arrived in the colony. We were all running now. With tambourines and drilled backs. I wanted to carry my vases, a roll of muslin. Sheep wool in baskets. Her hand was barely visible in the well of ink. Something in the lined sky. Strings and rain. A carnation and an avenue. You couldn't see the city from there. Velázquez wanted to ask me something about his palette, something foreign to him. The new archbishop. I went down again. I spoke kindly of Velázquez and his desires. I spoke of how he had run from the inquisition's plebeians. I told of how his manner would be welcomed by the King and Queen. Then they asked me of his lineage. They asked me about his penchant for light in broken shards. They asked me many things. Fire. Lake water. The alligator at the center of the earth. Cipactli and Cuauhtémoc. They asked me about earthen caldrons and the proper requirements for sacrifice. They whispered the words *Chac Mool* and pointed to a stream of vines and bouquets coming from the garden palace of the dead emperor. I was speechless. I was as always inside a register room, the accountant pleaded. Could I write down what had happened to Velázquez?

How could he have left all these gifts behind? Where will we go now that he has left us? The accountant screamed against the wall. There was very little left to do now. Sat back and thought of the Tallensi, African slave priests still in the kingdom. How they spoke of the circles above the mounds and how they used dung and sang to the ash spirits.

7

My leg stiffens. The crutch that holds me has become my aromatic rosary. My exact duplicate sits behind me. He wears the same sickness. The cabinet in front is halfway open. Dalí says that this is proper, that I should find the ecstasy on this shore, in the form of a wooden box, in Van Gogh's love for green boats sliced with bloody stripes.

The sea goes through me. I remember my mother's death this way: the last taxi in San José, the wrong street, 4th street to the abandoned apartments of the homeless instead of the hospital. This comes to me in times of quiet and rebelliousness.

Ten days the doctor said. Is she ready for her sacraments? the priest asked. We were in a mechanical room of hoses and meters, tubes and needles. I was sitting with her as she looked up for the last time. As I held her hand. What could we say at this time? What were the words worth? How could I apply the face cream holding itself inside the jar?

The horizon has a gospel. It sings for me far ahead where grayness becomes whiteness. I stretch out my right leg and place a handkerchief over my bad knee. My dead eye peeks through the furniture. Chucho and Velázquez, my cell brothers, wait for me. We wear the same clothes when the sea rolls out its bread. We pick up stones and scratch our names on sand. We sit bowed and astute. The replicas behind us do the same. Our dead mothers float far from where we sit. They drink from the green bottles still on their medicine chest. The little chest of drawers, the one that smells of apples and duck feathers.

8

She listened to Tjader on 22nd and faced fifty abstract pictures in her parents' dining room. At two yards they resembled the foreign mother and the frozen father. At one yard they resembled a jaguar, the god Ocelotl.

She walked into one chamber, the one where the jaguar eye becomes an eclipse between the realm of lost souls and the narrow passage to an asphalt strip and solar miracle where three living crystals speak eternity and powerlessness. Etched toothpicks on the cream, the yellow hair strands afloat on the table. The sea anemone by the bottom lip, a column of smoke over my mother's grave. Here, I walk.

Toward the land of Cibola, land of Zuñi treachery and Spanish greed. I hold her hand in mine, her soft whiteness and her lucid name, Aramara. Dare not pronounce it. I carry her inside and listen to her willed mantras. She says that in one or two more days, Cibola will contract and an earthquake will end the dominion's stronghold over America. She says that Cibola has grown too accustomed to the sea and the hair that circles its borders. They are prayers, they are incense from the tribute colonies. Tjader saves her, Tjader and the loaf of bread, Tjader and the chalice of apricot wine at the table. Two yards and tusks, three yards and a gypsy recites Lao Tzu's principle of force. Seventeen yards and the house resembles a checker-board. A Chagall in the chambers of Auschwitz, a wild blue horse baying without a neck or a body.

The Zuñi lift their hands in their usual stoic ways, they dance at the center of the table, with their soft arms curled around their bodies. Hands push out of the earth, eaten by ants and devoured by autos de fe, by Don Luis de Carvajal, the colonizer and governor of Nuevo León; they have been burned, you can tell by the way the ants travel around their bellies. Today they stand accused of harboring Jews. I travel northward. Behind Tjader. Cibola descends into the reddish lakes. A dog eats a crab and a calla lily erupts a shadow of a wild egg.

9

My daughter rests on the ledge to my left. In Phoenix, she says.
I've lived for many years in the land of the red tables. She stares
at her sisters. She calls them sisters.

She calls them nuns.
Waitresses from the Kalimba Café.

They honor her
or they sit at the base of the canyons
and worship each other. They hold up their busts,
eat sardines, and carve holes on the wall. Once in a while
they speak of Velázquez and his first voyage to Cuba.

They want to disobey the soldiers
on their next expedition to Yucatán.
My daughter is young, still. She fancies
the way the Golden Gate arches
over to the land of the Sausalitos.

I am a dancer from Kalimba,
she tells me.
Her headdress is revealing, a curled turban.
Wittgenstein looks to one side, he is not interested
in the arms pointing at him.

Wittgenstein has been uprooted by the villagers.
I am his consort, in a way. I am his accomplice
in a manner of speaking. Both of us look to one side
and neglect what is true and erotic.

We leave the flesh of things behind, we seek the air inside
the marrow, the capsule shaped lamps of Crete, made
out of pink stone and washed with Indian amaranth.

And yet, we snuggle to the sex slate,
below the orifice of the heavens.

The women have broken down the landscape
yet we seek fullness, we seek the second wall to come up again.
How silly to be held in such regard.

My daughter is from Kalimba,
she paints her breasts with berries and offers
dances to the red-haired God, Ocelotl.

10

They killed the Tlaxcalans. They slaughtered their daughters
and wept only once. When they were satiated with the scent
of *mazapán* after their sundry affairs in the harem,
this is when they wept.

Pulled out the robe of their ancestors from Extremadura and wept
aloud, as their banquets resumed in the gardens. I was left behind,
in the palace. In the military dance hall. I called to them once.

I wrote out the name of my gods in cuneiform, in the pink
negative language that I own from my mother, I scratched out
my own contract for transformation.

And yet, they issued the order against me.
It was simple and tawdry.
It was as usual. My skin was in their shape now. This was enough.
My skull resembled theirs, except my face
was bowed and fell into my chest,
in grayness. My arm resembled a loaf
of Spanish bread, my last breast
was held up for exhibition in the Friars' hallway. And my right hip
gashed with a capital letter. My legs folded in an odd fashion.
I could not speak.

Unrecognizable with my hands, with my letters
and the slit below my belly. A rag poured out of my bowels.
How they tried to clean me,

I don't know. A rag spilled
out of my back, how they tried to translate
my motion, who can say. The witnesses? The bartenders?

Ask Motolinía, ask Sahagún, ask my masters
lurking in these quadrants.

I have their clothes in my box. You can call them
and they will ask for trousers.
You can test the case if you wish. Only one arm holds me now.
I can't tell whose it is. It must be mine.

Recognize the strings that shoot from the ulna.
I can tell by the tattoo of a guacamaya parrot.
Sperm and seashells, yellow lines across my cheeks.
These are yours.

II

Of the sixty-two
viceroys who served in New Spain, three of them
had private Indian mistresses and fourteen of them had mulatto children.
They flayed skin and drank oyster juice.

They burnt corn tribute to Huitzilopochtli
in the name of Yahwe. I raise my arms to them.

Salud, I say. *Salud.* In the center of the table.
I can see their nakedness; this harpoon, I carry, in their accent.
This invention of being.

I must dive deep to find my father now.
In this office there is little to save except the disintegration
that plagues all species. I have learned to play the piano
and the clarinet. This is my new awareness.

I wear a bluish wig. I have learned to kneel
on water, outside where the old women loosen their clothes.
Ocelotl swishes his knife blade. He shows us his teeth.
The Central Valley coughs and fumbles for words.

How to describe this illusion:
in New York, the metros have rusted on their tracks.

Another homicide tells of this. Chiapas lives on bagels and tequila.
They know the history. They know
where to find the President's children.
They read Artaud in braille and rub their genitalia.

A sandwich, a Cezanne to mix things up a bit. Bologna or
ham on rye, garlic butter. More. Duck sauce and raspberry sausages.
Lobster, *ostión,* and *calabaza.* We must eat.

We must crash through our faces
and discover the new opening.

Eat the gold,
chew the strings, digest until we are ribbons,
reddish and jade green. Chinese and Vietnamese.
Cambodian and Hmong villages in tuxedos. Manila
and Northern Luzon where the Ilongot seek the words
for the new revolution.

12

First of all: cinnamon,

then turquoise.
First of all crimson powders,

then fire.

First of all, scars in braids across the back,
then colony, then origin, then you begotten in power.

You begotten in tranquillity. You in megalomania,
American new furniture.

You in blues and man in blue, in nails, in Madrid, with Juan Gris
drawing your nose and multiple eyes.

You, first of all in Diego Rivera's rogue trousers and boots.
First of all, you in thigh mambos. You in Erzuli's light captives
off the shores of Trinidad.

You marooned in Dutch ships.
First of all Zulu, first in Sudan, then Dinka.

First, the drum in the Sea of Cortez, across Janitzio, in Veracruz.
Tumbao, Chekere in octagons, crashed pubis and clenched bellies.
First, the feline stone in the portrait, the one where you reach for me,
without language, you say. Without the sludge and cottage industry
of apparitions for English trinkets.

First of all, Cha-Cha-Cha, then waves.
First, then second, Rumba, Queen of Cosmic Sweat, then night.
Do not believe this gutter guitar. This Velázquez, this time.

Do not believe it. Take the easel down. See through, for once.
See through Coptic, see through the Orange Free State,
the diamonds enlarged as penis and vulva.

I am in a half stance. One half goes into darkness with a rag of light
on my leg. The other half goes into you as you come to me,
as you march with your instruments and your continent,

blood soaked against your jacket,
tarnished by minstrel water.

13

The equator is close:
Rouge piano hearts of the peasants sing for me.

They ask me to come closer to my true beginnings. My arteries slip on the thin track that leads there. My mother's tiny hands swerve up toward the end point. My father's viscera engage me. He tells me, with one hand in the stomach, to pace myself.

Drink goat milk under the shelves, sprout your sea into this plenum. Crisscross and ink the dots. Attach the number 27 to the medulla, to the sacred eggs of Godadavida. This is the date when you were born. In a soft construction of morphine and agricultural gesticulations, in Central California, in Cibola. It is all in the sky now, elongated and cartoonish. Wavelengths from Portus Acapulco, the bishop's house at the mount. The few ships at the base are weary with his ambitions. Chucho el Roto has escaped from the *encomienda;* even though the town remains captive, in the hills, not far, we wait for a sign from the barracks where the last Chichimecs are allowed to wear Spanish arms. Is it my belly that wonders? Is it my tongue, outstretched in its grayish abandonment?

They have taken Gala to Vladivostok. She told me to follow the blue veins, to the yellow ones, these solar aches—to reach her. And yet, all I can do is cover myself in the strange foliage. Make marimbas out of the few tubers left in the ship, *La Caldea,* en route to the Philippines. Arpeggios. Pellets inserted into every pore.

I have contributed my forty-five days of labor. Blacks for sugar. Browns for added galley wash. The women stand in awe at our docile faces. My face has assumed a new air—sexual and transcendent bitterness. My thighs press against the railings, into grooves and Spanish masters. Syrup from our wombs grows sharp and distasteful. Who would have thought of such sweetness?

Who would have beheld such whiteness, ivory and rectangular boards besides our nakedness? In auction. In time, fashioned into the gaunt juice sacks of the warriors. Forty-five days again, I turn and sing. Forty-five pubis. Violet cream. Forty-five premature ejaculations in the chasms between Tiananmen and old Mexico.

I can see, from the balcony. The bulb, each new cleric's fingers, its tectonic stitches—potato carriers at the rim of the town squares. Smoke up through the cylinders and then sing the curdled fish slime. Who will pay off my debt? The belly eye sinks deeper into me. It caresses me with its new thinking. Tickles my insides. Brittle womb dolls, coiled. Gladiolas under boiling skin. Blotches from my past, come up from the tips of my breasts, my eyes and the points of my hidden hair. The vernacular is broken and full of stolen figures.

I will quote:
Sembla,
Ursa,
Minora,
Querétaro.

We are migrating to Prague, to Kafka's taciturn bedroom where he keeps a tray of wise apples to hurl at his hunched father. This is how to escape, he once told me. You take a tiny shred of gold, finished and grown secretly inside your laboratory. You take it and place it between your front teeth. Then, you stand, looking askance, as they pass by. Whistle to appear lazy. Yawn to appear intelligent. Soon enough you will move your face. The jaw will go back. The God Ocelotl will grant you one wish for having mimicked kindness.

15

The music comes from the Obraje.
From the textile mills in the center,
a bit to the right where the gold halo comes up.
Tiny solar lamps with a stern face.

I want to go out with my cassock my arm band in order, with my reddish
fruit tucked secretly beneath the folds. Sarajevo disagrees with me. She
insists that there is something eating at the center. Minute and dangerous,
she sings as she plays her fingers in the air, as she ducks from the bullets. In
the colony, I sit and listen to her admonitions. We made the finest cloth in
the colony, she says. Kerouac and Velázquez. The silk from China. Everyone
has contributed. Sarajevo comes out again with her bold chest draped in
blue. Riddled and caught in the dark angles of doors that break before us.

I can see her standing a few feet ahead of me. I cannot think how often she
has told me of her fortunes. The ones tattooed behind her knees. The
fortune of black lacquer, the broken asphalt mixed with tears after the
bombs. From here we can see her dangling from the mango trees. We run
to her, with stolen textiles, with robes jutting from our small vests. We
weave them at night and call to her.

The patch in the street that glows in the morning, the one with my father's
face. My uncle's face. Uncle Guzmán who at this very minute hides under
his bed waiting for death.

Last night I saw a blonde baby roll back into the chasms. I saved it, for a
second. Then she slid back into the concrete. Dwarf fire at her feet. Day in
day out. Sarajevo thinks of thrift. She thinks of holding the sleeves with her
teeth, the blue-black cabinets where the strings reside, the ones meant for
bread and dancing. I read the notes.

A man with gray hair and a long diplomatic back reads the notes. Sees
insects, production, industry, the court dockets of America. His back faces
me. I poke him with my cane. I push against his solid self, his little brothers
that oppress us.

Who are you? Bending at the jazz kitchen where they play Thelonius. Where they mash green doors on the piano keys. The pauses are significantly eternal. Police with crab suits. A Courbet above the door, framed in docile colors. Rag clouds in graffiti slime. Door is open.

This is all I have; an entrance to the kitchen, a fallow Stradivarius, wet with sputum and uterus. On top: the bridge puckers in Titian ochre. The torso, cut off. Lime water between the legs, tied and invented for the gaze jazz, the be-bop growl of someone standing like me. Congas, mambo skirts, a skull twisted into pleasure. This was our lot. At Tiananmen. Where we stood against the rectangles in green howl. This was our stance. Between a full line of Caruso and a wall of Auschwitz.

Build a guild, they told us. You must lay down the effigy. Gala must descend, she must be burned, they cried. But we held her up. In chalk dust. In a half-eaten dough ball, we carried her across the desert. This was our stance.

I looked for Sarajevo and Kerouac. Velázquez had escaped. We stood there at the tables of the new inquisition. Our ceramic pottery still showed evidence of Moorish influence. They used our bowls to serve the soldiers clean water.

Arabs and Jews,
in broken Macehual Aztec.

We stood there with Gala above us. They turned their engines on and mutilated our widows. They turned the engines on and fed us rice gruel. This was our stance, in that significantly short afternoon by the kitchen's tawdry piano keys.

The Consulado stood their ground. They left us no choice. I looked for the Infanta. She was our last hope. Ruffled in sky throat. The music was at our left, it was inside one of the Friars' dining halls. Full of reddish cabinets, strewn hair and cut fingers. I stood alone in front of the mad cylinders, for a second. A little girl in Spanish muslin was sliding into the drilling groove. I wanted to reach out for her. I wanted to pluck another note from the vented and grilled steel.

17

From the mad hills.
In burnt sienna and chopped Harleys.
Radishes in the bowels of the grilled pheasants—parsley and cauliflower.

The bluish knuckles work the maize dough, they work it into night. Stuffed sausages, prawn sauce. Cacao from the coast, banana and tiny potatoes, shriveled, dried and toasted. Incense rubbed on our thighs, with coriander braids and spearmint on our faces. Wash the belly with the orange heat from the persimmons, twist the sacred rinds at the small mounds spread across the last horizons. Michoacán, Cholula, Yemen.

Spanish bishops and followers of Zumárraga, protector of the moss children, the ones that walk in jazz beats and still bow to Tenochca and Ocelotl. More radish please, cranberry and corn rot for the dawn star.

We gather in a circle and follow the Smoke of the Tepo Drum with our sad ears and our wary hands. The women circle the fire. Shuffle the dust and spit to the left side. The champagne bottle remains in the Friars' domain, the one-eyed Dominicans. I whisper to Kerouac. He shuffles along with the Macehual women. He lays his belly on the map, the shallow mass graves dug out by the Criollos. Vladivostok, he points and shivers. St. Lara play your keys. Stroke our scars. Cling to our skirts, suckle our breasts, beat this last drum. Follow the ink to Portus Acapulco, to Tiananmen where we wait under the grills, in the one-celled housing. Where we sing with beehives and Gospel somnambulant Black sugar mill workers. I lay here. I lay with my arms arched across the anthills. They come to me, they speak in Mozart's infantile voice, they crawl into my ears and eat from the stolen honey I carry. They go down to my knees and crawl up to pubis. The black juice beats their triangle mouths. Frida's again, Georgia's. Gertrude's with asphalt wings. Pink powder, a lost boy with a holy wheel. Ezekiel, Joshua.

18

They want to root out the *conversos,* these Jews at my left. The Consulado searches for them. I laugh and kick the dust. I pick strawberry and plantain. No one knows their whereabouts. Like me. You in Freud's short coat, in Sarajevo's sweet rouge scarves. Chucho el Roto drinks his sack of wine. I know everything about the map. The spoiled code hidden in large cheese wheels, woven into secret hummingbird designs spun at the Obraje.

Drink and scrape the clay. Measure your words. Love the insects, note the jaw musculature. Listen to their watery sounds. Split sky, oven streets. A colonial tavern. And yet, who can discover the malady at work? Who can detect our sinew in the bread? Belly hair. That is all. Mustache wash, onyx sucked into the vagina. A cock, shaved and rubbed hot with anise and cinnamon. A tincture of cabernet, this ruby leather drop from the hungry nose. Siwanava, Goddess of Dead Children, I am calling you.

With my manicured black shoes, I draw your designs in the gravel. May the wind from Chiapas read my letters. The Catholic Kings cannot find me. They cannot pronounce me in this open seascape. I rest my large hands before your dinner table. I place them as soft constructions for your columns. For the angels that caress your oval-shaped ghosts.

19

In the sea with two miniature men. One on a rock, the other behind me. He is going down near Sarajevo. He wants me to reach the shore and greet tribes people. His arms cut into the waters, gently as if distilling the shafts of green, as if carrying a heavy briefcase. Notary sheets, stolen from the Holy Office. Muslin and algae wrap around my waist. My hands behind my head. I am looking for Chávez. My hidden mission. Chávez was with us from the beginning. He called the Roseworkers from the Obraje to lead a march against the Consulado. The rose patterns had been used to brand the natives without our knowing. Chávez knew this. The petals loomed at night and washed our dreams away. He lives at the bottom, between the reefs. He resembles the man to my right. Off center, with a sombrero and a broken back. With his legs bent and his head to one side. The sky doesn't answer our calls today. It is wet as the sea. It has been charged with sadness and readiness. We are the last ones on the shore. An odd day. The only alarming figure is the shore. With the head of a horse, with the teeth of a walrus. Hair down in old style, painted in umber and indigo strokes.

Where is the King? Why is this crown approaching my feet, so jagged and crystalline like sugar. Chávez appears diligent, armed with thorns.

20

Chávez has hurled me forward. The sky to the top left breaks and falls apart, into a turbulence. Then ochre and spleen. Then the vestibule below the heart. The empty trapezoid space where the heart used to be. This was my desire appearing to me in the desert. My arm was alone as my daughter's.

Someone had carved out my sacredness and instead filled me with a Vermeer, a Modigliani, a still and light colored vestment. These were my altar boy years, my cassock girl soliloquies. My arm was alone. One arm. They called it the arm of the Seeing Girl.

My ass, scaled, scalded, sits on a femur. A one-eyed cow and Freud graze next to my left thumb. The skin is horrible. The terms won't do well here. The phallus liver curls around my right thigh. And a clavicle, or is it my lost ulna, the one with ribbons—steps, if I could use that word—steps.

This is what Freud thinks. He thinks and paces the Spanish square. He counts the beans, my lonely chromosomes searching for my mother's grave. They want to go back, to crawl back to her physiologically incorrect womb, the one that shaped me, the one that encouraged my dreaming.

The split elbow resembles the sky, even if in dark sienna, even if in dark desolation. Da Vinci's hands, I want to say. The hands that shocked the Medicis in Rome. Why was I left standing in such a tragic manner? My full breast with its feverish nipple is an example of my own possibility toward rebirth. The brush strokes have marred me. My hair, my arching throat, my silk, woven across my skin. If I mention my foot, you mustn't ask any more questions.

Yes, this is my foot. I am sitting on it, seeking its milky chalk experience. The vestibule is out of context. This is where you must enter. This is where my being will be explained. How I arrived here. How I was dismembered. How I will reconstitute. How I have stood up high. How my fluid was drained. How love became disaster. How the fire was rearranged. How the bones were plastered with amaranth and roses. How the nose was smashed. How the little girl is contained inside the wrists. This is my secret: How the little girl is contained inside the wrists. How she managed to find a lover in the cinnamon-colored twists of smoke. The volcano may be of consequence, the one behind all of this, the one waiting for the small chapel to open or to fall, the chapel that looks upon me from afar.

21

Ocelotl, the red-haired god, has appeared. With the pelt of a sea lion leaning on a quarry of Carrara marble, to the right, where the speckled blood of the wars has worn down the landscape. Ocelotl leans forward with rubbery jaws, with the ears hidden. Our bright god waits calmly on the sand.

Ablutions and a hand raised to the sky are enough today. All the quicksilver from Cádiz has arrived, the sugar sacks in muslin from Córdoba lie at the dark feet of Ocelotl and yet the Jaguar Omen listens to the violins that García made. García, the wild eyed musician from the North. Composer of the pulque melodies for the Obraje, singer and long-haired minstrel of Sarajevo. She protects him, she answers his every prayer.

Today, in the dawn he was seen with the Trinity:
the Frida,
the Georgia,
the Gertrude.

The Trinity summoned Siwanava and spoke of Sarajevo's promise of exile and retaliation. They were holding up their fair skirts to the sky. Glass poured down. A bluish eye opened up from the thin Formica of the surrounding caves. I couldn't tell if they were singing or if they were burning the cloth, tossing it up into the air.

The Georgia had a reddish streak across her breasts, she said that it was her design for the new linen. Pedro Moya de Contreras would recognize it, she uttered. Moya would run into the cave and become mad. The Georgia stayed erect. The instruments at her feet curled. A French horn, a rough-hewn harp from the southern colonies, from the Land of Kerouac. El Paso was beyond the marble, beyond the caves—this is the direction where the Gertrude was singing as she played García's viola.

Yet, I couldn't see her legs, she was floating. A rose bush in heat was knotted around her throat, this was the sign of her powers. This was what

Pedro Moya de Contreras called sorcery. The Frida was close to my camp. I had seen her often, dragging a broken column, muttering about the whereabouts of Portus Acapulco, about Chucho el Roto and his scissors. She had told me that he was a liar and spendthrift, that his only gift was in escape and sabotage; the scissors were accessories to crimes against women at the Obraje. The Frida was close. An egglike being emanated from her forehead, woolly, whitish; a cotton mask of sorts, washed and brittle at the ends.

What was the music she was playing? A strange thick sound of falling keys, a syrup cry against sand and years of silence.

22

Sarajevo has been hit. Her limp hand has gone back, flipped into darkness. Only the shape of a colossal ink spill spreads across the lands. Or is it a woman with a beak and her arms up? All I can see are lines of black corn coming down from her bitten skirt and a continent blown out into archipelagos.

The little dream from the Pedro Moya de Contreras has come true it seems. Chávez has been detained again and García, the long-haired minstrel, has been taken captive.

The natural stone, the bread crust and the spleen are under a clean sky. The Goddess stands alone today. The Macehuales at the Obraje drink cabbage soup at break time, rub their thighs in order to remember the rose designs—everyone is still here under the new rule of the Consulado.

The Jews to my left and the Trinity; they slap against the fences but no one listens. Faces jut up from the dirt. Skeletons and half-skulls, eye orbits and smeared hair; smeared with feces and sperm.

A man hangs over the wires. They caught him this morning after attempting to find a new source for fire. Further back, next to the red girl, the girl that sings Kerouac, there is a dancer with her arms up. Her sleek back faces me. She lifts her face up toward the east. She says a man is being whipped by another man, on the side of fallen tree. Further back, she is gazing. Toward the new ashen, thin bluish sea. The rumble approaches; the rumble is Sarajevo's smoke. Igneous, metamorphic—male faces twisted in the gauze. Sarajevo's toast to the heavens.

23

The mortar shells rise up from cochineal, from vanilla, from the stolen hides—our tribute has not been enough. In the upward slopes that encircle us, they are coming and falling into sudden sadness and flatness. Van Gogh's favorite boats, in blood black, to my left.

Gala—no one knows her whereabouts. I know she has been here, swaying her hips and drinking her favorite cognac. The camel with a shrunken man rests at the horizon. A messenger? A shadow of loss and regret stalks the Obraje.

The tobacco monopoly keeps the Spanish in power. Who's to say when they'll draw their men out from our colonies. Who's to say that the sales tax will not keep on rising. Who sits around these figures and ponders? Instead they are building presidios in the north. Near Ensenada and the land of the Cocopá, my sisters of the Pacific. Yet the mortar shells continue as we continue in the Obraje. Isn't our labor enough? Count Regal and Count Valenciaga have taken all the gold from the mines. I can see them in their triangle clothes, with their hands in their pockets. Godadavida and Ocelotl remain in shards and pieces.

At night, in our *palmita,* in our small houses made of *bajareque,* we mix cereals and seed with blood from our tongues and ears and mash the pulp in old bowls from Ocosingo. We fashion small statues of the Goddess and the God of the Far and Near and we kiss their open breasts, we beat their heads with our little finger and ask them why and when and why and when? We breathe into them and ask them. O sisters, O Ensenada, the rooms here are resplendent with light. The fixtures are placed and the Macehual women await your arrival.

24

The anus. The apple.
The fork from Santander, the new colony for bee workers. The hand that
drips in the night.

The spoon from the anus of Valenciaga. The bone in the stocking shoot,
open bridal bread by the *tabla*. The collective masturbations of the
Bourbons. The anthill on the pubis, the whisker and the butter knife, the
ground opal dust still in the cabinet, the brown nipples severed and dried as
raisins, with cinnamon and coriander. The dragged bodies of the old
muscular women with thick torsos that drag grooves in the *mercados*
through the radish boxes and the avocados, the seventy-year-old man
hiding in the carcass of beef, the pig penis, screwed and basted in white
wine and garlic from Barcelona, Africa alone and unconquerable, alone in
the eyes of the Consulado, woman lips held up in the confiteor as a sign of
transcendence, the Jesuit friar sticking the fork under his ear to show us,
he repeats, that all these things are signs from his god.

After this passes, he says,
we will relocate to the mountains where they have a secret zoo and red
fields of fertile earth.

I want to call Gala.
I want to call the Trinity. Call Thelonius—this, I want to tell them,
this is ours.

25

The Consulado. After decades of names and quills, notaries and quipus knotted with our skin and hair, they have called Him into being.

He of the small mouth and large anus, he of the calling wire and the fast hand signs, as if he knew our songs, as if he knew our shuffle across the ash and the crests where we take cane flutes for the winds and place bitter eucalyptus and rosemary for the Ceiba deity, as if he knew how to angle the hands and dip them into the darkness, with weakness not strength, as if he knew the rose patterns of Chávez and the high thin voices of García's broken lyre made at San Juan Chamula and washed with pox, the nectar of the peasant students, as if he knew all this and the dark rings around our balché bowls in the circle of the night sweats and prayers, in front of the New Year God Pots, as if he knew this, he raises his hands in the shadow of Moya de Contreras, in the shadow of Valenciaga. He takes my daughter and her reddish figure of Ocelotl, he takes my son, the small boy who tunes church bells in the colony, who carves the proper names in the cereal figurines we make in the caves.

Sarajevo is my last resource. Bitten Sarajevo. Sarajevo of the limp hand stuffed inside her solar skirt. Is it time to call Margarita, the Infanta? Is it time to go back to her? Water, I ask. Water, first. Then, maybe rain. Maybe, an inverted tree with its ghost across my bed, to speak.

26

My childhood haunts me. It haunts me

with its jagged face rising up from the water, with its Hitler plate, so ready
to strike at the mother's round hand. My childhood faces the sea and wants
to turn into sand, into the gold from Cibola and Cadáquez. It wants to lay
back with its ruby juice opening its tiny valise.

Who can look into its timeless eye? Chucho? The old Tallensi sorcerers?
Who can measure the exact diameters inside its hollows, the velvet spiral
inside its Carrara? The noose and the apple float above my shoulders. The
foreign hips of the figure on the sand elude me.

A Macehual boy listens to Kerouac, he listens to Gala. Catalonia and
Rwanda swirl in the waters behind him. He is not in the chambers by the
horizon.

My childhood speaks, spellbound, and curls up. No one could own it if they
wished. In the colony, my childhood loses its slippers and climbs up a tree,
then a watermelon rind. The eye and the hand, in an ivory glow, in the folds
of a convex sky and a geometric draft of a feather—the eye and the hand
follow me wherever I go. The eye is kindness, the hand points down to the
inkwell and the champagne, to the Latin root of love. To the fixations of
Count Santiago de Calimaya; how he built a residence in New Spain and left
my mother sightless.

Engraved, etched, and hardened in the spleen; I search for my childhood. A
shrill whistle signals my findings. Above me in a bluish dome, the Count lies
dosing, thinking he has me captive. I drink and slobber his name.

27

The little boy breathes inside the mother. You can see through him too. His blonde head turns below us. And the shadows of his legs stretch across the Great Waters of Ensenada where his sisters live. He has been blessed. No one can dispute this. The Consulado throw up their hands. They have left it all to Pedro Moya de Contreras. Yet, all is well with the child. Sarajevo favors him.

Anise, amaranth, and eucalyptus from Catalonia, in a vial around his neck; this protects him. He floats in his mother's invisible vestments. An absolute cipher hangs on a string and guides him through the journey to America. A conch of talc and divine powder, a pebbled pattern on the skin of sea creatures contains his future instructions. Today marks his arrival into the colony. The child belongs to the Ocelotl God.

The stones part over his mother's grave. The brain in the air, the one floating with cauliflower designs and a tiny red missal, with a parchment inscribed with his songs; they wait for him to lift his head, for his mother to open her hands and Siwanava to blow through his rectangular lungs. The child's name is Zapata.

28

The story comes apart near Gala's eyebrows. This is where the plot shreds itself, where the foreign planet dissolves, the one with the face of Jupiter and the sky plagued by half-eyes—bacteria, with a shorn continent; half of Africa or was it half of Chiapas?

The lines of my face match her jugular; we both go up in an odd column, fast and folded. This language is futile, the letters empty themselves of the ink and the ink spills in rough circles and mythic shapes. I want to dream into them to find the next line or the next kiss. Alone this time. The Obraje and the Goddess have curled back into the air, the pulp inside the tree form, into the infinite staircase above Cadáquez in California.

If you hold your hand upright. If you spread the muslin mantle over the tabla. If you sit back for a second. If you raise your voice this time there will be a series of black dots in the mirror. Each one contains the ova for the next universe. No one knows how to decipher this today. No one except Zapata, the old Macehual sorcerer, the commoner who lives out his days in the hidden vault below Velázquez's cave. Velázquez told me this was his own secret. He said that he often spoke with Zapata. I am the one who feeds him fresh cut lamb shanks, he told me. Between my paintings, in the middle of sleep, I go to him and lift the small iron lid over his cell. I call out to him as candle light falls onto his face. I toss the meat to him and to the jaguar on the opposite chamber walled off by bars of Carrara. Zapata says that the mystery of our lives depends on the spatter of dots and glyphs on the jaguar's yellow pelt, he says it depends on the motion of these figures as the Great Omen paces in the wet darkness. Zapata has the face of a woman, Velázquez said. The lips, the tresses.

Beneath Your Skin

Beneath Your Skin

A strange sharp whitish black—you whisper to me
something like centimeters continents, the waning night
is smoke, it is a whip that swings in your arms, stone.
No one really re-cognizes you. Your skin, for
example, is a clasp of nuns on fire or earthquakes
ships lamps open covers from a sexual honey,
an invisible (as always) heat. A reddish
summer sheet. Every number on your throat.
Whirlwinds
Velvet
An arrow coming at you
We sweat and we bathe in our mid-flight
Oval hair Everything that will never
be said on the Mount
since it is so evident divine me.

Bajo tu piel

Bajo tu piel

Una extraña blancura negra filosa—me estás murmurando
algo como centímetros continentes—la noche menguante
es humo, es látigo que se columpia en tus brazos, piedra.
Nadie realmente te re-conoce. Tu piel, por
ejemplo, es un ramillete de monjas encendidas o de sismos
barcos lámparas amplios manteles de una miel
sexual, un calor (como siempre es) invisible. Sábana
guinda de verano. Cada número en tu garganta.
Remolinos
Terciopelo
Flecha hacia ti
Sudamos y nos bañamos en medio de nuestro vuelo
Óvalo cabellera Todo lo que nunca
se dirá en el Cerro
por ser la letra tan clara adivíname.

About the Author

Juan Felipe Herrera's recent books include *Border-Crosser with a Lamborghini Dream, Thunderweavers/Tejedoras de rayos, Lotería Cards & Fortune Poems* (illustrated by Artemio Rodriguez), *Crashboomlove,* and *The Upside-Down Boy/El Niño de Cabeza.* He is Professor of Chicano and Latin American Studies at California State University, Fresno. He lives in Fresno with his soul partner, performance artist and poet Margarita Luna Robles.